The

SMUCKER'S

Cookbook

SMITHMARK

Contents

Introduction   9

Appetizers   11

Main Dishes

    Beef   14

    Lamb   17

    Pork   19

    Poultry   22

    Fish and Seafood   25

Vegetables and Salads   28

Sauces and Chutneys   32

Breads   34

Cookies   40

Desserts   44

Beverages   57

Index   60

Introduction

The J.M. Smucker Company, founded in 1897 and still managed by members of the Smucker family, is the largest producer of jams, jellies, preserves, ice cream toppings, and fruit syrups in the United States. Only the finest ingredients and the highest quality fruits are used in Smucker's products.

The recipes in this book include old favorites as well as imaginative new dishes. They all have one thing in common — each recipe's special flavor comes from Smucker's fruit products. Appetizers, main courses, salads, vegetables, sauces, beverages, breads, and desserts are all enriched by the sweet and tangy addition of Smucker's preserves, jellies, toppings, or fruit syrups.

Appetizers

Dressed-Up Cheese Dollars *7 to 8 dozen*

½ pound sharp Cheddar cheese, grated
1 cup butter or margarine, softened
2 cups sifted all-purpose flour

¾ to 1 cup Smucker's® Blackberry Jelly

In a bowl, combine cheese and butter. Cream together until blended. Add flour gradually, mixing with a spoon until all ingredients are well blended. Refrigerate until firm. Form into 3 rolls, each 1 inch in diameter. Wrap in waxed paper. Refrigerate several hours or overnight. Preheat oven to 425° F. With a sharp knife, cut cheese rolls into slices about ¼ inch thick. Place ½ inch apart on ungreased baking sheets. Bake 8 to 10 minutes, or until lightly browned. Cool 10 minutes. To serve, spread one dollar with jelly, top with second dollar. (See photo, page 13.)

Sweet-and-Savory Sausage Balls *50 appetizers*

Easy to make the day before—refrigerate, then reheat just before serving.

1 pound bulk pork sausage
1 cup Smucker's Cider Apple Butter
½ cup Smucker's Sweet Orange Marmalade

3 tablespoons lemon juice
¼ teaspoon salt
½ teaspoon ground ginger

Form sausage meat into balls about ¾ to 1 inch in diameter. Place in a shallow baking pan. Bake 15 minutes in a 400°F oven, or until thoroughly cooked. Drain on paper towels. Combine remaining ingredients and heat over low heat until marmalade is melted. Add sausage balls and simmer 15 minutes. Serve hot from chafing dish or over a candle warmer.

Appetizer Meatballs   *about 50 meatballs*

1 pound ground beef	*All-purpose flour*
¾ teaspoon salt	*2 tablespoons butter or margarine*
2 tablespoons finely minced onion	*1 cup Smucker's Peach Preserves*
½ cup fresh bread crumbs	*¼ cup prepared horseradish*
¼ cup milk	*2 teaspoons dry mustard*

Combine ground beef, salt, and onion. Combine bread crumbs and milk and add to meat mixture. Toss lightly until well blended. Form mixture into tiny meatballs about ¾ inch in diameter. Roll meatballs lightly in flour. Heat butter in skillet and brown meatballs well on all sides. Drain off excess fat. Combine preserves, horseradish, and dry mustard; blend until smooth. Add to meatballs in skillet; reduce heat and simmer 8 to 10 minutes, stirring occasionally, until all meatballs are glazed. Serve from a chafing dish or over a candle warmer.

Good Idea: *For a change in flavor, omit preserves, horseradish, and dry mustard, and heat meatballs with a combination of ½ cup Smucker's Sweet Orange Marmalade, 1½ teaspoons curry powder, and ⅛ teaspoon onion salt.*

Dunkers' Delight   *12 servings*

1 cup Smucker's Pineapple Preserves	*2 eggs, well beaten*
¼ cup prepared mustard	*1 cup water*
¼ cup prepared horseradish	*1½ teaspoons salt*
2 to 3 cups cooking oil	*3 tablespoons sesame seed*
6 whole chicken breasts, skinned and boned	*1 cup all-purpose flour*

In a saucepan, combine preserves, mustard, and horseradish. Heat over low heat until well blended. Keep sauce warm. Fill a skillet no more than half full of oil; heat oil to 375° F. Cut chicken into 1- × 1½-inch pieces. Combine eggs, water, salt, sesame seed, and flour. Dip chicken pieces into batter, draining off excess. Place in oil. Fry 3 to 5 minutes, or until golden brown. Drain on paper towels. Keep warm in warm oven. Dip into reserved sauce.

Good Idea: *Bring these hot to a snack table if you like; keep the sauce hot over a candle warmer.*

Raspberry Frost (page 59), Appetizer Meatballs,
Dressed-Up Cheese Dollars (page 11)

Main Dishes
Beef

Sauerbraten *10 to 12 servings*

1½ cups vinegar
1½ cups water
2 bay leaves
12 whole cloves
1½ teaspoons salt
¼ teaspoon pepper
¼ teaspoon ground mace
1 tablespoon sugar

2 large onions, sliced
¼ cup cooking oil
4-pound top or bottom round of beef
¼ cup all-purpose flour
3 tablespoons shortening
¾ cup gingersnap crumbs
½ cup Smucker's *Peach Preserves*
½ teaspoon ground ginger (optional)

In a large saucepan, combine vinegar, water, bay leaves, cloves, salt, pepper, mace, sugar, and onions. Bring to a boil. Cool; add oil. Place meat in a deep glass or china bowl. Pour vinegar mixture over meat. Place in refrigerator and let stand 2 to 4 days, turning meat once a day so it will marinate evenly. Remove meat from marinade and pat dry with paper towels. Dust surface of meat with flour. Melt shortening in heavy Dutch oven; add meat and brown well on all sides. Add marinade. Cover tightly and simmer over low heat 3 to 4 hours, or until meat is fork-tender. Turn meat occasionally during cooking time. Remove meat to a hot serving platter and keep warm. Strain marinade. Return 2 cups of the strained marinade to Dutch oven. Add gingersnap crumbs and preserves. Simmer until mixture is thick and smooth. Add the ginger, if desired. Cut meat in slices; serve with sauce.

Good Idea: *For a different flavor, thicken marinade with 3 tablespoons flour blended into ¼ cup water, rather than with gingersnap crumbs. Stir in ½ cup Smucker's Grape Jelly. When smooth and thick, stir in ½ cup dairy sour cream. But whichever flavor you prefer, serve potato dumplings or potato pancakes, and red cabbage—they are go-togethers for sauerbraten.*

Sauerbraten, Red Cabbage (page 31)

Glazed Beef Brisket *8 to 10 servings*

4 to 5 pounds, beef brisket
1 medium onion, quartered
8 peppercorns
1 teaspoon salt

¾ cup Smucker's Apricot Preserves
2 teaspoons lemon juice
1 teaspoon salt
Whole cloves

Place meat in a large kettle and cover with water. Add onion, peppercorns, and 1 teaspoon salt. Cover tightly and simmer 3 to 4 hours, or until meat is tender. Remove meat and place in a shallow baking dish. Combine preserves, lemon juice, and 1 teaspoon salt. Spread half of glaze over top of meat. Stud meat with cloves. Bake, uncovered, in a 350° F oven 20 to 30 minutes, or until glaze is set. Heat remaining glaze and serve with meat. (See photo, page 33.)

Good Idea: *This brisket is even better the second day. Serve cold, in thin slices, with the remaining sauce heated, or serve with any of the other sauces for cold meats on page 32. Save the good broth in which the meat was cooked—freeze it, if you like—to be used in soups or stews.*

Spicy Short Ribs *4 to 6 servings*

3 pounds short ribs of beef
¼ cup all-purpose flour
2 tablespoons shortening
1 cup beef broth or bouillon
½ cup Smucker's Apricot Preserves
2 tablespoons brown sugar

2 tablespoons vinegar
¼ teaspoon ground allspice
¼ teaspoon ground cinnamon
¼ teaspoon ground cloves
1 tablespoon cornstarch
1 tablespoon cold water

Remove as much fat from ribs as possible. Dust ribs with flour. Melt shortening in a Dutch oven or large heavy skillet. Place ribs in skillet; brown well on all sides. Pour off excess drippings. Combine broth, preserves, brown sugar, vinegar, and spices. Pour over ribs. Cover and cook over low heat about 2½ hours, or until ribs are tender, turning ribs occasionally. With a spoon, skim as much fat as possible from top of sauce. Combine cornstarch and water to make a smooth paste. Stir into sauce and cook, stirring, until sauce is clear and lightly thickened.

Good Idea: *This is particularly good made a day in advance. Do not thicken. Refrigerate and, when cold, remove all fat from top of sauce and meat. Just before serving, heat, then thicken with cornstarch paste as above. Mashed potatoes are just right with these ribs and their tasty sauce.*

Sweet-and-Sour Meatballs   *6 to 8 servings*

1 cup fresh bread cubes	¼ teaspoon pepper
1 cup milk	2 (12-ounce) bottles chili sauce
2 pounds ground beef	1 cup Smucker's *Grape Jelly*
⅓ cup finely chopped onion	½ cup water
1 egg	1 cup dairy sour cream
1 teaspoon salt	Hot cooked noodles

Soak bread cubes in milk. Combine with ground beef, onion, egg, salt, and pepper. Shape mixture into balls about 1 inch in diameter. In large saucepan, combine chili sauce, jelly, and water; heat to simmering. Drop meatballs into hot sauce and simmer gently about 1 hour. Skim off excess fat. Just before serving, add sour cream to sauce and heat, but do not boil. Serve on a bed of hot cooked noodles.

Lamb

Special Skewered Lamb   *6 servings*

2 tablespoons butter or margarine	⅛ teaspoon cayenne pepper
2 large onions, finely chopped	2 tablespoons curry powder
½ clove garlic, minced	¼ cup vinegar
1 cup Smucker's *Apricot Preserves*	2 pounds lean leg of lamb, cut into
¼ cup Smucker's *Apricot Syrup*	1-inch cubes
1 teaspoon salt	

Melt butter in saucepan. Add onions and garlic; cook until limp. Add preserves, syrup, salt, cayenne pepper, curry powder, and vinegar. Cover and simmer gently until well blended. Add lamb cubes to sauce and refrigerate several hours or overnight. Stir occasionally. Drain meat; thread on skewers at least 6 inches long. Place on broiler rack and broil about 10 minutes to desired degree of doneness, turning occasionally. Heat remaining sauce over low heat to serve with meat.

Good Idea: *This is especially good cooked over hot coals. Squares of green pepper and button mushrooms can be added to the meat on the skewers, if you like.*

Currant Roast Lamb   *8 to 10 servings*

1 5- to 6-pound leg of lamb, boned
½ cup Smucker's *Currant Jelly*
2 cups fresh bread crumbs
¼ cup chopped celery
3 tablespoons butter or margarine,
   melted

⅛ teaspoon pepper
¼ teaspoon ground allspice
½ teaspoon salt
2 tablespoons brown sugar
1 teaspoon ground nutmeg
Jelly Sauce (follows)

Spread leg of lamb out as flat as possible; spread with jelly. Combine bread crumbs, celery, butter, pepper, and allspice. Spread over jelly. Fold lamb over to enclose stuffing and tie with string every 4 or 5 inches. Place fat side up on a rack in a shallow roasting pan. Combine salt, brown sugar, and nutmeg. Sprinkle over top of lamb. Roast in a 325° F oven about 2 hours or to a temperature of 175° to 180° F on a meat thermometer. Cut lamb in slices and serve with Jelly Sauce.

Jelly Sauce   *about 2 cups*

½ cup Smucker's *Currant Jelly*
¾ cup water
¼ cup firmly packed brown sugar
6 tablespoons lemon juice

½ teaspoon salt
¼ teaspoon ground nutmeg
⅛ teaspoon ground allspice
⅛ teaspoon pepper

In a saucepan, combine all ingredients. Heat over low heat, stirring constantly, until jelly melts and sauce is hot. Serve with slices of roast lamb.

Grape Lamb Chops   *6 servings*

2 tablespoons cooking oil
6 small shoulder lamb chops
   (1¾ to 2 pounds)
1 medium onion, minced
½ cup ketchup

½ cup Smucker's *Grape Jam*
1 tablespoon Worcestershire sauce
1 teaspoon salt
1 tablespoon prepared mustard
Hot cooked rice

Heat oil in a large skillet. Add lamb chops; brown on both sides. Remove chops and set aside. Add onion to drippings in skillet; cook just until soft but not browned. Add ketchup, jam, Worcestershire sauce, salt, and mustard. Blend well. Return chops to skillet. Cover tightly and simmer about 1 hour or until chops are tender, turning chops occasionally. Remove cover during last 15 minutes of cooking time to reduce liquid. Serve with hot cooked rice.

Pork

Pork and Peppers *4 servings*

4 large green peppers, cut into
  1-inch squares
1 egg
2 tablespoons all-purpose flour
½ teaspoon salt
⅛ teaspoon pepper
1 pound very lean pork, cut into
  1-inch cubes

½ cup cooking oil
1 small clove garlic, minced
1 cup chicken broth or bouillon
2½ tablespoons cornstarch
2 tablespoons soy sauce
¼ cup vinegar
½ cup Smucker's *Pineapple Topping*
Hot cooked rice

Place pepper chunks in boiling water 2 to 3 minutes. Drain and reserve. Combine egg, flour, salt, and pepper. Add pork cubes to batter and toss lightly with a fork so that each piece of pork is coated. Heat oil in heavy skillet. Add garlic and cook 1 minute. Add pork and cook until golden brown, about 5 to 6 minutes. Pour off as much oil as possible. Add ⅓ cup of the broth to skillet. Cover and simmer 10 minutes, or until pork is tender. Combine remaining broth, cornstarch, soy sauce, vinegar, and topping. Add to skillet and cook, stirring constantly, until mixture thickens and becomes clear. Stir in reserved green pepper and heat thoroughly. Serve immediately with hot cooked rice.

Pork-Kraut-Apple Skillet *6 servings*

6 lean pork chops, cut ¾ inch thick
1 tablespoon cooking oil
1 teaspoon salt
2 tablespoons butter or margarine

3 large onions, thinly sliced
¾ cup Smucker's *Cider Apple Butter*
2 pounds sauerkraut, drained
1 cup diced, unpeeled apple

Remove as much fat as possible from the chops. Heat oil in a large, heavy skillet. Season chops with salt; place in skillet and brown on both sides. Remove chops. Melt butter in skillet; add onions and cook 1 minute. Add apple butter and blend. Return chops to skillet. Cover tightly and simmer about 30 minutes. Combine sauerkraut and diced apple and place on top of chops. Cover and simmer, stirring occasionally, about 20 minutes, or until chops are tender. (See photo, page 21.)

Good Idea: Add a loaf of good dark bread, with plenty of butter, to make a complete, hearty one-dish meal. If desired, the sauerkraut and apples can be cooked separately, then garnished with additional apples. Serve with pork chops and apple butter.

Pineapple Spareribs   *5 to 6 servings*

---

3 to 4 pounds lean spareribs
1 cup Smucker's *Pineapple Preserves*
¼ cup vinegar

½ cup ketchup
1 tablespoon soy sauce

Cut ribs into serving pieces. Arrange half the pieces in a single layer in a roasting pan. In a saucepan, combine preserves, vinegar, ketchup, and soy sauce. Heat, stirring constantly, until well blended. Pour half the pineapple mixture over the layer of ribs. Top with remaining ribs and remaining pineapple mixture. Cover pan and bake in a 350° F oven 1½ hours. Uncover and continue baking 20 to 30 minutes, basting with the pineapple mixture occasionally, until ribs are brown and tender.

Good Idea: *For a change in flavor, try Smucker's Peach Preserves in this recipe—it's equally good!*

Spicy Plum-Sauced Ham   *9 to 12 servings*

---

1 3- to 4-pound canned ham
1 cup Smucker's *Plum Preserves*
½ cup chutney, chopped

2 teaspoons wine vinegar
1 tablespoon sugar
⅛ teaspoon ground mace

Place ham on rack in a shallow roasting pan. Roast in a 350° F oven 1½ to 1¾ hours, or until heated through. In a saucepan, combine remaining ingredients and heat over low heat, stirring until well blended. Use to baste ham during last 15 minutes of cooking time. Heat remaining sauce and serve with slices of ham.

Good Idea: *For smaller hams, decrease roasting time and for larger hams, increase roasting time. The amount of sauce remaining to serve with slices will depend on the size of ham used and on how heavily the ham is basted during cooking time.*

Strawberry Ham Steak   *2 to 3 servings*

---

2 tablespoons prepared mustard
½ cup Smucker's *Strawberry Topping*

1 pound fully cooked ham steak, cut 1 inch thick

Combine mustard and topping. Place ham steak on rack in broiler pan. Broil about 5 inches from heat 12 to 15 minutes, turning once and brushing frequently with topping mixture.

Pork-Kraut-Apple Skillet (page 19)

Poultry

Curried Orange Chicken   *4 servings*

1 cup Smucker's *Sweet Orange*
  Marmalade
1 tablespoon curry powder
1 teaspoon salt

½ cup water
1 broiler-fryer, quartered or cut into
  serving pieces

Butter a 9- × 13-inch baking pan. Combine marmalade, curry powder, salt, and water. Place chicken pieces, cut side down, in pan. Spoon marmalade sauce over chicken and bake, uncovered, in a 350° F oven 45 minutes. Spoon sauce over chicken several times during cooking. If sauce begins to stick to bottom of pan, add an additional ¼ cup water. Remove chicken. Pour out sauce and skim off fat. Serve sauce hot with chicken.

***Good Idea:** Buttered noodles seem just right with this dish. Garnish both noodles and chicken with parsley for a pretty touch. (And always encourage the family to eat the garnish—parsley is rich in vitamins.)*

Peach-Glazed Chicken   *6 to 8 servings*

2 broiler-fryers, cut into serving pieces
½ teaspoon salt
1 cup Smucker's *Peach Preserves*

1 orange, juice and grated peel
2 tablespoons minced crystallized ginger
1 teaspoon curry powder

Sprinkle chicken with salt. In a saucepan, combine remaining ingredients; heat over low heat. Place chicken in a shallow baking pan, skin side down. Brush with preserves glaze. Bake uncovered in a 400° F oven 25 minutes, basting often with glaze. Turn chicken over. Bake 30 minutes longer, continuing to baste with the glaze, until chicken is tender. Brush remaining glaze on chicken just before serving.

***Good Idea:** If you don't have crystallized ginger, substitute ½ teaspoon ground ginger—the texture will be different, but the flavor just as good.*

Cherry-Roasted Chicken   *4 servings*

1 (5-ounce) package brown and wild
   rice mix
⅓ cup Smucker's *Cherry Preserves*
½ cup chopped celery
1 broiler-fryer (3 pounds)
2 tablespoons butter or margarine,
   melted

¼ cup minced onion
1½ teaspoons curry powder
1 cup Smucker's *Cherry Preserves*
1 teaspoon grated orange peel
¼ cup orange juice

Cook rice mix according to package directions. Add ⅓ cup preserves and celery and mix well. Stuff chicken with rice mixture; close openings, tie drumsticks to tail, and tuck wings under back. Place breast side up on rack in shallow roasting pan. Brush with half the melted butter. Roast uncovered in a 375° F oven 1 hour. While chicken is roasting, cook onion in remaining butter until tender. Add curry powder and blend. Add remaining 1 cup preserves, grated orange peel, and orange juice. Simmer 2 minutes, stirring occasionally. Roast chicken 30 minutes longer, or until tender, brushing several times with sauce. Heat remaining sauce and serve with chicken and stuffing.

Apricot Chicken   *4 servings*

Chicken and fruit preserves make great partners—here is a particularly flavorful way to combine them.

½ cup Smucker's *Apricot Preserves*
2 tablespoons soy sauce
1 tablespoon lemon juice
¼ cup minced onion

1 tablespoon chopped parsley
⅛ teaspoon oregano
1 broiler-fryer, cut into serving pieces

In a flat glass or china dish or in a mixing bowl, combine preserves, soy sauce, lemon juice, onion, parsley, and oregano. Add chicken pieces and turn several times, coating them well with sauce. Refrigerate overnight, turning pieces several times. Remove from sauce and place in a single layer in a baking pan. Bake, uncovered, in a 375° F oven 45 to 50 minutes, or until chicken is tender and lightly browned. Brush with sauce several times during cooking. Brush remaining sauce on chicken just before serving.

Good Idea: *This is particularly nice with hot cooked rice. The sauce tops the rice and adds to the tastiness.*

Fish and Seafood

Sweet-Sour Fish Sticks *3 to 4 servings*

¼ cup cooking oil	2 tablespoons grated onion
¼ cup lemon juice	1 teaspoon dry mustard
½ teaspoon salt	½ cup Smucker's *Currant Jelly*
½ teaspoon pepper	1 pound frozen fish sticks

In a small saucepan, combine oil, juice, salt, pepper, onion, dry mustard, and jelly. Heat gently, stirring occasionally, until jelly melts and mixture is blended. Place fish sticks on a heatproof broiling platter. Brush fish sticks heavily with sauce. Broil about 4 inches from source of heat for 3 minutes. Turn, brush heavily with sauce. Broil 3 to 5 minutes, or until tops are lightly browned and bubbly. Baste once again during cooking time, if desired. Serve with remaining sauce, reheated.

Batter-Fried Shrimp *6 servings*

2 eggs	2 teaspoons cooking oil
½ cup milk	2 pounds fresh or frozen whole shrimp
1 cup all-purpose flour, stirred before measuring	Oil or shortening for deep-fat frying
1 teaspoon baking powder	Orange Sauce (follows)
1 teaspoon salt	Plum Hot (follows)

Beat together eggs and milk until frothy. Sift together flour, baking powder, and salt. Add to egg mixture; add oil and beat until mixture is smooth and well blended. Set aside. Remove shells from shrimp, leaving tails on. If shrimp are frozen, remove shells under running cold water. Cut partway through, lengthwise along outside curve. Lift out vein; wash shrimp and flatten so they stay open. Drain well on paper towels. Place enough oil or shortening to more than cover shrimp in a deep-fat fryer or kettle and heat to 375° F. Dip shrimp into batter, one at a time, and fry, a few at a time, about 4 minutes, or until golden brown and puffy. Drain on paper towels. Serve immediately with Orange Sauce, or Plum Hot. (See photo, page 27.)

Orange Sauce   *about 1 cup*

1 cup Smucker's *Sweet Orange*
   Marmalade
1 clove garlic

1 piece whole ginger root or ½ teaspoon
   ground ginger

In a small saucepan, combine all ingredients and cook over low heat, stirring constantly, until mixture bubbles. Remove garlic and ginger root. Serve with Batter-Fried Shrimp.

Plum Hot   *about 1 cup*

1 cup Smucker's *Plum Preserves*
1 to 2 cloves garlic, as desired, very
   finely minced

2 teaspoons soy sauce
¼ teaspoon pepper

In a small saucepan, combine all ingredients and cook over low heat, stirring occasionally, at least 5 minutes, or until garlic is cooked. Remove from heat and cool slightly. Serve with Batter-Fried Shrimp.

Good Idea: With these shrimp and their delicious sauces, try serving brown rice cooked with onion, green pepper, and chopped mushrooms. For dessert, lemon or lime sherbet seems just right—offer some crisp cookies, too.

Sweet-and-Pungent Shrimp   *3 to 4 servings*

3 tablespoons brown sugar
2 tablespoons cornstarch
½ teaspoon salt
1 tablespoon soy sauce
¼ cup vinegar
¼ teaspoon ground ginger
¾ cup Smucker's *Pineapple Preserves*

¾ cup water
1 green pepper, cut into thin strips
1 onion, thinly cut and separated into
   rings
1 pound fresh or frozen shrimp, cleaned
   and cooked
Hot cooked rice

In a saucepan, combine sugar, cornstarch, and salt. Add soy sauce, vinegar, ginger, preserves, and water. Cook mixture over medium heat until thickened, stirring constantly. Add green pepper and onion; simmer 2 minutes. Add shrimp. Bring to a boil, stirring constantly, and cook until shrimp are hot. Serve immediately with hot cooked rice.

Batter-Fried Shrimp (page 25), Orange Sauce, Plum Hot

Vegetables and Salads

Pat's Apricot Mold *8 to 10 servings*

½ cup Smucker's *Apricot Preserves*
½ cup Smucker's *Pineapple Topping*
2 tablespoons vinegar
2½ cups water
1 teaspoon whole cloves

4-inch stick cinnamon
2 (3-ounce) packages orange flavor
  gelatin
½ cup dairy sour cream

In a saucepan, combine preserves, topping, vinegar, and water. Tie cloves and cinnamon in a small square of cheesecloth and place in saucepan. Simmer mixture over low heat 10 minutes. Remove spice bag. Dissolve 1 package gelatin in 2 cups of the liquid. Stir until dissolved. Pour into a 6-cup mold and refrigerate until almost firm. Meanwhile, dissolve second package of gelatin in remaining preserve mixture and stir until dissolved. Refrigerate until partially set. Whip with a rotary beater until fluffy. Fold in sour cream. Pour mixture over first layer in ring mold. Refrigerate until firm, about 8 hours or overnight. Unmold to serve.

Good Idea: *This is an all-purpose dish. It can be the main course of a light luncheon. It can come to the dinner table as a salad to accompany the meat. And in a pinch—perhaps with an added dollop of sour cream—it could serve as dessert.*

Yams Baked in Marmalade Sauce (page 30),
Spiced Beets (page 31)

Yams Baked in Marmalade Sauce   *6 servings*

7 medium yams (2 to 2½ pounds)
½ cup firmly packed brown sugar
½ cup Smucker's *Sweet Orange Marmalade*

3 tablespoons butter or margarine, melted

Wash yams. Cover and cook in boiling water 20 to 30 minutes, or until tender. Cool. Peel yams, cut into quarters, and arrange in single layer in shallow baking dish. Combine brown sugar, marmalade, and butter, and pour over yams. Bake, uncovered, in a 400° F oven 20 to 25 minutes, basting and turning yams frequently so they glaze on all sides. (See photo, page 29.)

Good Idea: *If you're in a hurry, use drained canned yams in this dish—2 (1-pound 8-ounce) cans will work perfectly in this recipe.*

Grandma's Baked Squash   *4 servings*

Try preparing acorn squash this way as a change from the more usual butter-and-brown-sugar seasoning.

2 medium-size acorn squash
2 tart red apples, diced
½ cup chopped nuts

½ cup Smucker's *Apple Jelly*
¼ cup butter or margarine, softened

Cut squash in half lengthwise; scoop out centers. Place in baking pan. Combine apples, nuts, jelly, and butter. Fill squash with mixture. Pour a small amount of boiling water in pan around squash. Cover pan with foil. Bake in a 400° F oven 45 to 60 minutes, or until fork-tender. Remove foil during last 5 minutes of baking.

Orange-Pineapple Cole Slaw   *4 servings*

2 medium oranges
½ cup mayonnaise
½ cup Smucker's *Pineapple Topping*

¼ teaspoon salt
4 cups finely shredded cabbage

Peel oranges. Over medium bowl, with a small sharp knife, cut between orange sections. Reserve sections, discard membrane. Add mayonnaise, topping, and salt to juice in bowl; stir to blend well. Add cabbage and orange sections and toss lightly. Refrigerate at least 1 hour before serving. (See photo, page 33.)

Spiced Beets *3 to 4 servings*

2 tablespoons butter or margarine
1 small onion, thinly sliced
1/2 teaspoon salt
1/8 teaspoon pepper
1/2 teaspoon ground cinnamon

1/4 teaspoon ground ginger
3 tablespoons lemon juice
1/4 cup Smucker's *Sweet Orange Marmalade*
1 (1-pound) can sliced beets, drained

Melt butter in saucepan. Separate onion slices into rings. Reserve a few rings for garnish; place remaining rings in saucepan. Cook over medium heat 2 minutes. Add salt, pepper, cinnamon, ginger, lemon juice, and marmalade. Bring to a boil. Add beets; cover and simmer over low heat about 5 minutes. To serve, garnish beets with reserved onion rings. (See photo, page 29.)

Glazed Carrots *6 servings*

1 1/2 pounds carrots, cut into
    1/4-inch slices
1/3 cup Smucker's *Peach Preserves*

3 tablespoons butter or margarine
1 tablespoon lemon juice
1 tablespoon snipped parsley

Cook carrots, covered, in a small amount of boiling salted water about 10 minutes, or until tender. Drain thoroughly. Add preserves, butter, and lemon juice, and cook over low heat, stirring occasionally, until butter is melted and carrots are evenly glazed and heated. Sprinkle with parsley just before serving.

Red Cabbage *6 servings*

1 small head red cabbage
    (1 1/2 to 2 pounds)
3 tablespoons butter or margarine
1 medium onion, chopped
1/4 cup vinegar

1/2 cup water
1/2 cup Smucker's *Currant Jelly*
1 1/2 teaspoons salt
1/8 teaspoon pepper
1/2 cup seedless raisins (optional)

Remove core and shred cabbage coarsely. In a large saucepan, melt butter; add onion and cook about 3 minutes or just until soft. Add cabbage, vinegar, and water. Cover and simmer about 10 minutes, or just until cabbage is crisp tender. Add jelly, salt, pepper, and raisins, if desired; toss lightly. Cook, uncovered, over low heat until cabbage is well glazed and hot. Serve with sauerbraten, pork, or hamburger patties. (See photo, page 15.)

Good Idea: *Smucker's Cherry Preserves in place of Smucker's Currant Jelly makes a very pleasant flavor change.*

Sauces and Chutneys

Hot Mint Sauce *about ¾ cup*

½ cup Smucker's *Mint Flavored*
   Apple Jelly

2 tablespoons lemon juice
2 tablespoons grated lemon peel

In a saucepan, combine all ingredients and heat gently, stirring constantly, until jelly is melted. Serve hot with any lamb dish.

Plum Chutney *about 2 cups*

1 cup Smucker's *Plum Preserves*
3 tablespoons wine vinegar
1 teaspoon ground ginger

1 teaspoon ground mace
1 cup seedless raisins
1 cup chopped pecans

Combine all ingredients. Let stand several hours to blend flavors. Serve with cold meats or with curry dishes.

Apple Chutney *about 1½ cups*

1 cup Smucker's *Apple Jelly*
½ cup seedless raisins
½ cup slivered blanched almonds

1 small tart apple, peeled and chopped
1 teaspoon lemon juice

Combine all ingredients; let stand at least 1 hour to blend flavors. Serve with cold meats or with any curry dish.

Plum Chutney, Apple Chutney, Picture-Pretty Bread (page 37)
Orange-Pineapple Cole Slaw (page 30), Glazed Beef Brisket (page 16)

Breads

Jelly-Glazed Sally Lunn *1 loaf*

½ cup milk
½ cup butter or margarine, softened
¼ cup sugar
1 teaspoon salt
½ cup warm water (105–115°F)
1 package active dry yeast

3 eggs
3½ to 4 cups all-purpose flour,
*   stirred before measuring*
¼ cup Smucker's *Grape Jelly*
2 tablespoons chopped blanched
*   almonds (optional)*

Heat milk until small bubbles appear at edge; add butter, sugar, and salt. Cool to lukewarm. Into a large, warm bowl, measure water (it should feel comfortably warm when tested on inside of wrist.) Sprinkle in yeast; stir until dissolved. Add lukewarm milk mixture, eggs, and 3 cups flour; mix well, then beat until well blended. Add enough additional flour (½ to 1 cup) to make a stiff batter. Cover with waxed paper and a towel; let rise in a warm place until doubled in bulk, about 1 hour. Grease and flour 9- or 10-inch bundt or tube pan. Stir batter down and beat well, about ½ minute. Place batter in prepared pan. Smooth surface by patting with lightly floured fingers. Cover and let rise in warm place until doubled in bulk, about 1 hour. Preheat oven to 350° F. Bake 9-inch loaf 45 minutes, or until loaf sounds hollow when tapped with fingers. For 10-inch loaf, reduce baking time 10 minutes. Remove from pan and place on rack. Melt jelly in a saucepan over low heat. Let cool to thicken slightly, then spoon over top of loaf. Sprinkle chopped almonds on top, if desired. Serve warm, in thick slices, with additional jelly. Use a serrated knife to slice, or pull loaf apart into thick "slices" with two forks.

Jelly-Glazed Sally Lunn,
Breakfast Blossoms (page 36),
Orange Marmalade Bread (page 36)

Breakfast Blossoms *9 rolls*

*1 package refrigerated snowflake dinner
    rolls (9 rolls)*
*¾ cup Smucker's Sweet Orange
    Marmalade*

¼ teaspoon ground cinnamon
¼ teaspoon ground nutmeg

Preheat oven to 375° F. Grease nine 2½- or 3-inch muffin pan cups. Separate dough into 9 rolls. Separate each roll into 5 even sections or leaves. Place 1 leaf in the bottom of each muffin cup. Stand 4 leaves around edge of cup, overlapping slightly. Press dough edges firmly together. Repeat with remaining leaves. Combine marmalade, cinnamon, and nutmeg. Place a rounded tablespoonful of the mixture into the center of each cup. Bake 10 to 12 minutes, or until lightly browned. Cool slightly before removing from cups. Serve warm. (See photo, page 35.)

Good Idea: You can also use refrigerated butterflake dinner rolls. Divide dough into 12 rolls. Separate each roll into 3 even sections or leaves. Place 1 leaf in the bottom of each muffin cup, stand 3 leaves around edge of cup, and proceed as above. Or try placing the dinner rolls upright in muffin cups, as directed on the package. Slightly separate tops of rolls and fill crevices with marmalade before baking. For flavor variation, try Smucker's Peach Preserves with ¼ teaspoon ground nutmeg and ⅛ teaspoon ground ginger, Smucker's Cherry Preserves with ⅛ teaspoon almond extract, or Smucker's Blueberry Preserves with ⅛ teaspoon ground cinnamon.

Orange Marmalade Bread *1 loaf*

*3 cups all-purpose flour, stirred before
    measuring*
4 teaspoons baking powder
1 teaspoon salt
½ cup chopped walnuts
2 eggs, lightly beaten

2 tablespoons cooking oil
¼ cup honey
*¾ cup Smucker's Sweet Orange
    Marmalade*
¾ cup milk

Preheat oven to 350° F. Grease a 9- × 5- × 3-inch loaf pan. Into a large bowl, sift together flour, baking powder, and salt. Stir in nuts. Combine eggs, oil, honey, marmalade, and milk; blend well. Add to flour mixture; stir only until flour is well moistened (batter will be lumpy). Turn batter into prepared pan. Bake 65 to 70 minutes, or until lightly browned and a tester inserted in center comes out clean. (See photo, page 35.)

Picture-Pretty Bread *1 loaf*

1 cup warm water (105–115°F)
1 package active dry yeast
¼ cup Smucker's *Sweet Orange Marmalade or Apricot or Peach Preserves*
2½ cups all-purpose flour, stirred before measuring

¼ cup nonfat dry milk solids
2 tablespoons wheat germ
2 tablespoons whole bran
1 teaspoon salt
1 tablespoon cooking oil

Into a large, warm bowl, measure water (it should feel comfortably warm when tested on inside of wrist). Sprinkle in yeast; stir to dissolve. Stir in marmalade or preserves; let stand 5 minutes. Combine 1 cup flour with dry milk, wheat germ, bran, and salt. Add to yeast mixture; stir until well mixed. Stir in oil and remaining flour to make a soft dough. Turn out onto a floured board and knead until smooth and elastic. Place in a greased bowl; turn dough over to grease top. Cover and let rise in a warm place, free from draft, until doubled in bulk, about 1 hour. Turn out of bowl onto a board, knead slightly, and shape into a ball. Let stand 20 minutes. Grease a 9- × 5- × 3-inch loaf pan. Shape dough into a loaf and place in prepared pan. Cover and let rise in a warm place, free from draft, until doubled in bulk, about 45 minutes. Preheat oven to 350° F. Bake 50 to 60 minutes, or until bread sounds hollow when tapped. Turn out onto a rack and cool thoroughly before slicing. (See photo, page 33.)

Saucer Pancakes *6 servings*

Some people call these "Dutch Babies"—whatever you call them, they're very good and very pretty.

6 eggs
1 cup milk
1 cup all-purpose flour, stirred before measuring
½ teaspoon salt

¼ cup butter or margarine, melted
1 cup Smucker's *Red Raspberry or Plum Jelly*
Confectioners' sugar
1 lemon, cut into 6 wedges

Butter 6 individual shallow casseroles or skillets that are 6 to 7 inches in diameter. Preheat oven to 400°F. In a medium bowl, beat together eggs and milk. Add flour and salt; beat until smooth. Stir in butter. Fill each prepared casserole with about ½ cup batter. Bake 20 minutes. Reduce heat to 350° F and bake another 5 to 10 minutes, or just until dough is firm. Serve immediately, topped with jelly and a sprinkling of sugar; a lemon wedge should accompany each, to be squeezed over just before the pancake is eaten. (See photo, page 39.)

Griddle Cakes   *3½ dozen*

2 cups all-purpose flour, stirred before
    measuring
3 teaspoons baking powder
2 tablespoons sugar
1 teaspoon salt
3 tablespoons butter or margarine,
    melted

1 egg
1½ cups milk
Butter or margarine
Smucker's *Strawberry or Blueberry*
    Syrup

Into a medium bowl, sift together flour, baking powder, sugar, and salt. Combine melted butter, egg, and milk; blend well. Pour over dry ingredients and blend until smooth. Preheat griddle until hot. Grease lightly. Drop batter by tablespoonfuls onto griddle. When a few holes appear around sides of pancake and bottom is browned, turn and brown other side. Serve immediately with butter and fruit syrups.

Good Idea: *If batter is allowed to stand about 30 minutes before baking, it will mellow. Then, when pancakes are baked, bubbles will appear on the surface, which is a signal that it is time to turn the cake.*

Swedish Pancakes   *6 servings*

A Swedish pancake pan can be purchased at a good specialty shop—be sure to follow manufacturer's directions for seasoning the pan.

2 eggs
3 cups milk
1⅓ cups all-purpose flour, stirred before
    measuring
1 tablespoon sugar

1 teaspoon salt
Melted butter or margarine
1 cup Smucker's *Blueberry Preserves or*
    Blackberry Jam

Beat together eggs and milk. Add flour, sugar, and salt; beat until smooth. Heat Swedish pancake pan slowly. Brush with melted butter. Stir batter, pour into depressions in pan, and bake until browned on one side. With small spatula, turn cakes to brown other side. Cakes should be thin with crisp edges and delicately browned all over. Arrange 6 hot pancakes in a circle on a warmed plate and serve hot with preserves or jam.

Good Idea: *If you do not have a Swedish pancake pan, drop batter by tablespoonfuls onto a heated griddle. Cook quickly. Serve with preserves or jam—for breakfast or lunch, or as dessert after a light dinner. This will make about 6 dozen thin pancakes.*

Saucer Pancakes (page 37), Swedish Pancakes, Griddle Cakes

Cookies

Jelly-Nut Thumbprints *about 2 dozen*

½ cup butter or margarine
½ cup firmly packed light brown sugar
1 egg
1½ cups all-purpose flour,
   stirred before measuring

1 egg white, lightly beaten
1 cup finely chopped nuts
¾ to 1 cup Smucker's *Strawberry, Black
   Raspberry, or Cherry Jelly*

Cream butter and sugar together until light and creamy. Beat in egg. Stir in flour and mix until thoroughly blended. Refrigerate dough to chill slightly, about 1 hour. Preheat oven to 350° F. Grease baking sheets. With floured hands, roll dough into balls 1 inch in diameter. Dip balls into egg white, then roll in chopped nuts. Place cookies 2 inches apart on baking sheets. With a thimble, the handle of a wooden spoon, or your thumb, make a depression in center of each cookie. Bake 10 to 12 minutes, or until lightly browned. Cool cookies on rack. If centers have risen during baking, press down again while cookies are hot. When cool, fill centers with jelly. (See photo, page 43.)

Jennie's Special Ladyfingers *2 dozen*

1 (3-ounce) package cream cheese,
   softened
¼ cup Smucker's *Blackberry Jam*

2 dozen ladyfingers
Confectioners' sugar

Combine cream cheese and jam and blend thoroughly. Split ladyfingers; spread bottom halves with jam mixture. Replace tops; sprinkle with confectioners' sugar.

Good Idea: *For a flavor change, try Smucker's Apricot Preserves and a little chopped candied ginger blended with the cream cheese.*

Grape-Nut Triangles *4½ dozen*

*1½ cups all-purpose flour,
    stirred before measuring*
½ teaspoon baking powder
⅛ teaspoon salt
¾ cup sugar
½ cup butter or margarine
1 egg

½ teaspoon vanilla extract
1 tablespoon milk
½ cup Smucker's Grape Jelly
¼ cup chopped pecans
¼ cup flaked coconut
Confectioners' sugar

Into a medium mixing bowl, sift together flour, baking powder, salt, and sugar. With a pastry blender or two knives, cut butter into mixture to the consistency of cornmeal. Combine egg, vanilla, and milk; add to crumb mixture and mix until well blended. Refrigerate dough 2 hours. Combine jelly, pecans, and coconut. Let set until ready to use. Preheat oven to 350° F. Lightly grease baking sheets. On a floured board, roll out half the dough at a time to about a ⅛-inch thickness. Cut into 2-inch squares. Place about ½ teaspoonful of jelly mixture in center of each square. Fold into a triangle, pressing edges together. Repeat with remaining dough. Place triangles on baking sheets. Bake 10 minutes, or until lightly browned. Remove to rack to cool. When cool, sprinkle with confectioners' sugar.

▼▲▼

Berrybush Christmas Cookies *100 cookies*

1 cup butter or margarine
½ cup sugar
1 egg yolk
½ teaspoon salt
*2½ cups all-purpose flour,
    stirred before measuring*

4 egg whites, at room temperature
¼ teaspoon cream of tartar
10 tablespoons sugar
¾ cup ground walnuts
1 cup Smucker's Blackberry Jelly
1 cup chopped walnuts

Preheat oven to 350° F. Cream butter and ½ cup sugar together until light and fluffy. Stir in egg yolk. Stir together salt and flour; stir into mixture. Pat dough into thin layer in bottom of a 15- × 10- × 1-inch jelly-roll pan. Bake 20 minutes. Beat egg whites with cream of tartar until stiff but not dry. Add 10 tablespoons sugar gradually, continuing to beat until mixture stands in stiff peaks. Fold in ground walnuts. Spread jelly over top of partially baked dough in pan. Spread egg white mixture over top of jelly. Seal edges. Sprinkle meringue with chopped walnuts. Bake 10 to 15 minutes, or until lightly browned and set. When cool, cut into 1- × 1½-inch rectangles.

Good Idea: *Serve these with punch at a party. Other flavors of jelly, such as Smucker's Red or Black Raspberry or Strawberry, are also tasty in these cookies.*

Grandmother's Jelly Cookies

1 cup butter or margarine, softened
1½ cups sugar
1 egg
1½ teaspoons vanilla extract

3½ cups all-purpose flour,
  stirred before measuring
1 teaspoon salt
½ to ¾ cup Smucker's *Red Raspberry Jelly*

In a large bowl, cream together butter and sugar until light and fluffy. Add egg and vanilla; beat well. Stir in flour and salt; mix well. Stir (if batter gets too hard to handle, mix with hands) to make a smooth dough. Refrigerate about 2 hours. Preheat oven to 375° F. Lightly grease baking sheets. On a lightly floured board, roll out half of dough to about a ⅛-inch thickness. Cut with a 2½-inch cookie cutter. Roll out remaining dough, but cut with a 2½-inch cutter with a hole in the middle. Place on baking sheets. Bake 8 to 10 minutes, or until lightly browned. Cool about 30 minutes. To serve, spread jelly on plain cookie; top with a cookie with a hole.

Sandbakkelse   *about 2 dozen*

Make these buttery Norwegian cookies in pans purchased in specialty stores, or use 2½-inch tart or muffin pans.

1 cup butter or margarine, softened
1 cup sugar
1 egg

2 cups all-purpose flour,
  stirred before measuring
½ cup finely chopped blanched almonds
1 cup Smucker's *Strawberry Preserves*

Preheat oven to 350° F. Grease and lightly flour sandbakkelse pans. In a medium bowl, cream together butter and sugar until light and fluffy. Beat in egg. Stir in flour and almonds; mix until thoroughly blended. Press mixture onto bottom and sides of prepared pans, using about 2 tablespoonfuls of mixture per cup and making a ⅛- to ¼-inch layer. Cut off top edges evenly. Bake 15 to 20 minutes, or until lightly browned. Turn pans upside down on a cooling rack and let stand until cooled slightly. Tap pans lightly to loosen cookies; finish cooling on rack. Fill centers with about 2 teaspoons preserves.

Good Idea: *For a fancy dessert, fill cookies with whipped cream flavored with almond extract, and top with a dab of preserves.*

Grandmother's Jelly Cookies,
Jelly-Nut Thumbprints (page 40)

Desserts

Aunt Dilla's Jelly-Icing Cake   *12 servings*

²/₃ cup shortening
1 cup sugar
3 eggs
2 cups sifted cake flour
3 teaspoons baking powder

½ teaspoon salt
½ cup milk
1 teaspoon vanilla extract
Whipped Jelly Icing (follows)

Grease bottoms of two 8-inch round cake pans. Fit circle of waxed paper in bottom of each pan and grease again. Set aside. Preheat oven to 350° F. Cream shortening; add sugar and beat until light and fluffy. Add eggs one at a time, beating well after each addition. Sift together flour, baking powder, and salt. Combine milk and vanilla. Add alternately with flour mixture, starting and ending with flour mixture and beating well after each addition. Divide batter between prepared pans. Bake 25 to 30 minutes, or until cake springs back when touched lightly with fingertips. Let stand in pans about 5 minutes. Turn out of pans onto rack and cool. Put layers together with Whipped Jelly Icing and frost top and sides of cake.

Whipped Jelly Icing

1 cup Smucker's *Currant or Black*
   Raspberry Jelly

2 egg whites
⅛ teaspoon salt

Combine all ingredients in top part of double boiler. Cook over boiling water, beating constantly with rotary beater or electric mixer, until mixture stands in stiff peaks. Makes enough frosting for tops and sides of two 8- or 9-inch layers.

Aunt Dilla's Jelly-Icing Cake,
Jelly Roll (page 46)

Downside-Up Cherry Cake *8 servings*

¼ cup butter or margarine, softened
¾ cup Smucker's *Cherry Preserves*
1⅓ cups all-purpose flour,
  stirred before measuring
2 teaspoons baking powder
⅔ cup sugar

½ teaspoon salt
2 eggs
½ cup milk
¼ cup butter or margarine, melted
1 teaspoon vanilla extract
Cream (optional)

Preheat oven to 350° F. Spread softened butter in a 9-inch round cake pan. Spread preserves over top of butter. Sift together flour, baking powder, sugar, and salt. Beat together eggs, milk, melted butter, and vanilla. Add to dry ingredients and stir just until mixture is smooth. Pour over preserves in cake pan. Bake 20 to 25 minutes, or until lightly browned. Let stand 2 to 3 minutes. Turn upside down on serving dish. Let stand a few minutes so preserves will drain out over top of cake. Remove pan. Serve warm, with whipped cream, if desired.

Jelly Roll *10 servings*

1 cup sifted cake flour
1 teaspoon baking powder
¼ teaspoon salt
3 eggs
1 cup sugar

⅓ cup water
1 teaspoon vanilla extract
Confectioners' sugar
1 cup Smucker's *Blackberry or*
  Elderberry Jelly

Grease a 15- × 10- × 1-inch jelly-roll pan. Line the bottom with waxed paper and grease again. Preheat oven to 375° F. Sift together flour, baking powder, and salt. In a medium bowl, beat eggs until thick and pale in color. Gradually beat in sugar; continue beating until stiff. Beat in water and vanilla. Mix in dry ingredients and beat just until batter is smooth. Pour into prepared pan. Bake 12 to 15 minutes, or until lightly browned. Loosen edges and immediately turn cake upside down on a tea towel that has been sprinkled with confectioners' sugar. Carefully peel off paper. Cut away crisp edges of cake. While it is still hot, roll up cake and towel from the narrow end. Cool on cake rack. Unroll cake and remove towel. Spread cake with jelly and roll up again. Sprinkle with additional confectioners' sugar before cutting into slices for serving. (See photo, page 45.)

Pumpkin Marmalade Tarts (page 48),
Strawberry-Cheese Pie (page 50), Peach Tarts (page 49)

Pineapple Cheese Pie   *6 to 8 servings*

2 teaspoons cornstarch
2 tablespoons sugar
1 cup small-curd creamed cottage
   cheese
2 eggs, separated
2 tablespoons milk

⅛ teaspoon salt
1 tablespoon grated lemon peel
1 tablespoon lemon juice
¾ cup Smucker's *Pineapple Preserves*
1 unbaked 9-inch pastry shell

Preheat oven to 450° F. Combine cornstarch and sugar. Add cottage cheese and blend well. Stir in egg yolks, milk, salt, lemon peel, and lemon juice. Beat egg whites until stiff but not dry. Fold into cheese mixture. Spread preserves over bottom of pastry shell. Pour cheese mixture over preserves. Bake 10 minutes. Reduce heat to 350° F; continue baking 25 to 30 minutes, or until filling is set. Refrigerate at least 2 hours before serving.

Pumpkin Marmalade Tarts and Pie   *12 servings*

Here's a new way with an old favorite to try at holiday time—as a bonus, there is extra filling for a pie that can go into the freezer.

1 (1-pound) can or 2 cups pumpkin
1 cup Smucker's *Cider Apple Butter*
3 eggs
½ cup firmly packed brown sugar
2 tablespoons cornstarch
1 teaspoon ground cinnamon
¼ teaspoon ground nutmeg

¼ teaspoon ground ginger
1⅔ cups evaporated milk
12 unbaked 3-inch pastry shells
1 unbaked 8-inch pastry shell
¼ cup sugar
½ cup Smucker's *Sweet Orange
   Marmalade*

Preheat oven to 425° F. Combine pumpkin and apple butter; blend well. Separate 2 of the eggs and reserve 2 egg whites. Beat together the 2 egg yolks and the whole egg. Add to pumpkin mixture. Blend in brown sugar, cornstarch, and spices. Add milk; blend well. Pour ¼ cup of the pumpkin mixture into each 3-inch pastry shell. Pour remaining mixture into 8-inch pastry shell. Bake 15 minutes. *For pie,* reduce heat to 325° F and continue to bake about 25 minutes, or just until set. Cool. *For tarts,* reduce heat to 325° F and continue to bake 10 to 15 minutes, or just until set. Do not overbake. Remove from oven. Beat egg whites until stiff. Gradually beat in sugar until mixture is very stiff. Spoon 2 teaspoons marmalade over top of each tart. Spread tops with meringue, being sure to seal edges. Bake tarts 10 to 15 minutes longer at 325° F, or until meringue is lightly browned. Cool. Serve tarts, or refrigerate until serving time. When pie is cooled, wrap in moisture-vaporproof wrap and freeze. (See photo, page 47.)

Good Idea: If the tarts don't appeal to you, use two unbaked 8-inch pastry shells, and divide the filling between them. Bake both pies until custard is set. Spread one pie with ¼ cup marmalade, then with the meringue, and bake until meringue is browned. Freeze the second pie for later use. When used, thaw at room temperature and top with marmalade and meringue as with first pie and bake until meringue is browned. Or, if desired, serve thawed pie topped with whipped cream.

Peach Tarts *12 servings*

Here's an easy-to-do dessert with a subtle "what's that?" flavor that will have everyone guessing.

2 eggs, well beaten
2 cups dairy sour cream
½ teaspoon vanilla extract
¼ teaspoon almond extract

1 cup Smucker's *Peach Preserves*
12 unbaked 3-inch pastry shells
Toasted slivered almonds

Combine eggs, sour cream, and vanilla and almond extracts; blend well. Fold in preserves. Spoon mixture into pastry shells. Sprinkle tops with almonds. Bake in a 350° F oven 25 to 30 minutes, or until mixture is set. Refrigerate at least 2 hours before serving. (See photo, page 47.)

Brownie Pie A La Mode *8 servings*

Chocolate lovers, attention—here's the dessert that you've been waiting for.

2 cups (1 pint) vanilla ice cream,
  slightly softened
1 (15½-ounce) package brownie mix
½ cup chopped walnuts

½ cup Smucker's *Chocolate Fudge*
  Topping
2 tablespoons flaked coconut

Spoon ice cream into chilled 2-cup bowl or mold, packing it firmly with back of spoon. Cover with plastic wrap or foil and freeze until very firm. Prepare brownie mix according to package directions, adding walnuts while mixing. Bake in 9-inch pie plate. Cool completely. To serve, remove ice cream from freezer. Dip bowl in lukewarm water for 5 seconds. Cut around edge of ice cream with knife and invert onto center of brownie pie. Pour topping over ice cream; sprinkle with coconut. Let stand 5 to 10 minutes at room temperature. Cut in wedges to serve.

Strawberry-Cheese Pie   *6 servings*

2 (3-ounce) packages cream cheese,
    softened
¼ cup light cream
1 baked 9-inch pastry shell, cooled

1 quart ripe strawberries, washed and
    hulled
½ cup Smucker's *Strawberry Jelly*

Combine cream cheese and cream; beat until light and fluffy. Spread over bottom of pastry shell. Arrange strawberries, points up, over top of cream cheese mixture. Melt jelly over low heat, stirring constantly. Cool slightly, then spoon over top of strawberries. Refrigerate to chill well before serving. Cut with a sharp knife. (See photo, page 47.)

Sundae Puffs   *6 servings*

¼ cup butter or margarine
½ teaspoon salt
½ cup water
½ cup all-purpose flour,
    stirred before measuring
2 eggs

1 (5-ounce) package vanilla pudding
    and pie filling mix
2½ cups milk
¾ cup Smucker's *Chocolate Fudge
    Topping*

Preheat oven to 400° F. Grease a baking sheet. In a large saucepan, combine butter, salt, and water. Bring to a boil. Add flour all at once and cook over medium heat, stirring constantly, until mixture leaves sides of pan and forms a ball of dough. Remove from heat and add eggs, one at a time, beating well after each addition. Continue beating until mixture is smooth and glossy. On prepared baking sheet, form dough into 6 mounds at least 2 inches apart. Bake 30 to 35 minutes, or until puffs are high and lightly browned. Remove from oven and turn off heat. Make a slit in the side of each puff to allow steam to escape. Return puffs to oven and let stand about 10 minutes with oven door open. While puffs are baking, combine pudding mix and milk in a saucepan. Cook over medium heat, stirring constantly, until mixture thickens and comes to a boil. Pour pudding into a bowl, cover with a piece of waxed paper, and refrigerate until chilled. Just before serving, split puffs and fill bottoms with pudding. Replace tops of puffs and spoon topping over each.

Good Idea: *On another occasion, fill puffs with a favorite ice cream and top with Smucker's Chocolate Fudge Topping or Strawberry Preserves. To make eclairs as shown in the photograph, shape dough with a spatula on a greased baking sheet into 6 fingers about 1 × 4 inches. Bake same as puffs.*

Caramel Flan   *6 to 8 servings*

⅓ *cup* Smucker's *Caramel or
    Butterscotch Flavor Topping*
*1 (8-ounce) package cream cheese,
    softened*

½ *cup sugar*
1 teaspoon vanilla extract
6 eggs
2 cups milk

Butter a 9-inch round cake pan that is at least 1½ inches deep. Pour topping into pan. Beat together cream cheese, sugar, and vanilla until smooth. Beat in eggs, one at a time, until light. Blend in milk. Pour mixture carefully into pan. Set pan in a larger baking pan. Pour in boiling water to a depth of ½ inch. Bake in a 350° F oven 50 minutes, or just until set in the center. Do not overcook. Remove from hot water bath and cool on a rack for 10 minutes. With a sharp knife, loosen edge of custard. Invert cake pan onto a large dinner plate with a rimmed edge or a well in the center. Let stand a few seconds. Remove pan and spoon any remaining topping over custard. Refrigerate 2 to 3 hours before serving.

Good Idea: The topping is so tasty and adds so much to the flavor that serving some extra topping, cold or warmed, with the flan makes this good dessert even better.

Marmalade-Walnut Baked Apples   *6 servings*

---

6 medium baking apples
½ *cup* Smucker's *Sweet Orange
    Marmalade*

¼ *cup chopped walnuts*
¾ *cup* Smucker's *Red Raspberry Syrup*

Wash and core apples. Starting at stem end, peel apples ⅓ of the way down. Arrange apples in a shallow baking dish, peeled sides up. Combine marmalade and walnuts, and fill centers of apples with mixture. Pour syrup over apples. Bake in a 350° F oven 50 to 60 minutes, or until apples are easily pierced with a fork. Spoon syrup in dish over tops of apples frequently during baking time. Let apples stand 5 minutes. Spoon sauce in bottom of dish over tops of apples once more for a lovely shiny glaze.

Good Idea: If you prefer to let the good marmalade flavor stand alone, omit raspberry syrup and baste apples during baking with a simple syrup made of ¾ cup sugar and 1 cup water, boiled together 10 minutes before serving.

Strawberry Ice Cream   *about 1½ quarts*

1½ cups milk
1 tablespoon cornstarch
⅛ teaspoon salt
2 eggs

1 cup Smucker's *Strawberry Syrup*
½ cup Smucker's *Strawberry Preserves*
1½ cups heavy or whipping cream

In a saucepan, combine milk and cornstarch. Cook over moderate heat, stirring constantly, until mixture comes to a boil. Simmer 1 minute. Beat salt and eggs together. Stirring constantly, add about half of the hot milk mixture to eggs. Return mixture to saucepan. Cook over low heat, stirring constantly, for 1 minute. Remove from heat and stir in syrup and preserves. Refrigerate about 1 hour, or until chilled. Stir in heavy cream. Process according to your ice cream freezer directions.

Good Idea: *For a change of flavor, omit Smucker's Strawberry Preserves and Syrup; substitute Smucker's Seedless Red Raspberry Jam and Red Raspberry Syrup. And, for a quick treat on a day when you're in a hurry, have a sundae party with vanilla ice cream from the store, served with a selection of several syrups and toppings.*

Nutted Grape Sauce   *about 1½ cups*

½ cup Smucker's *Grape Jam*
1 tablespoon lemon juice

½ cup Smucker's *Pineapple Topping*
½ cup chopped pecans or peanuts

In a saucepan, combine jam, lemon juice, and topping. Cook over low heat, stirring constantly, until jam melts. Remove from heat and cool. Stir in nuts. Serve over cake squares with ice cream.

Grape Dessert Sauce   *about 3 cups*

2 cups Smucker's *Grape Jelly*
½ cup Smucker's *Apricot Syrup*
½ cup orange juice

2 teaspoons lemon juice
¼ teaspoon ground nutmeg

In a saucepan, combine all ingredients. Cook over low heat, stirring constantly, until jelly melts. Serve warm over ice cream, cake squares, pancakes, or waffles.

Sundae Party—Vanilla Ice Cream
with Smucker's Toppings

Frozen Strawberry Pie   *6 to 8 servings*

1⅓ cups vanilla wafer crumbs
½ cup finely chopped pecans or walnuts
⅓ cup butter or margarine, softened
½ cup Smucker's *Strawberry Preserves*

½ cup Smucker's *Strawberry Jelly*
1 egg white
1 cup dairy sour cream
Sliced fresh strawberries (optional)

Combine crumbs, nuts, and butter. Press firmly on bottom and sides of 9-inch pie plate. Bake in a 350° F oven 8 to 10 minutes. Cool. In small bowl of electric mixer, combine preserves, jelly, and egg white; beat 5 to 10 minutes at high speed, until soft peaks form. Gently fold in sour cream. Spoon mixture into prepared shell. Freeze pie until firm; serve frozen. Garnish pie with a few sliced fresh strawberries before serving, if desired.

Cheesecake Sensation   *12 to 14 servings*

The combination of flavors is what makes this cheesecake sensational—that, and the sink-all-through goodness of the syrup.

¼ cup graham cracker crumbs
4 (8-ounce) packages cream cheese,
  softened
4 eggs
1¾ cups sugar

2 tablespoons lemon juice
2 tablespoons grated lemon peel
1 teaspoon vanilla extract
½ cup Smucker's *Apricot Syrup*
½ cup Smucker's *Strawberry Preserves*

Butter inside of straight-side casserole or soufflé dish 8 inches wide and 3 inches deep. *Do not use a springform pan.* Sprinkle with graham cracker crumbs and shake around the bottom and sides until coated. Set dish aside. Combine cheese, eggs, sugar, lemon juice, grated lemon peel, and vanilla. Beat at low speed, and as ingredients blend, increase speed to high, scraping the bowl several times. Continue beating until thoroughly blended and smooth. Pour and scrape batter into prepared dish; shake gently to level mixture. Set dish inside a slightly wider pan; add boiling water to larger pan to a depth of about ½ inch. Do not let edge of cheesecake dish touch rim of larger pan. Bake in a 325° F oven 1½ to 2 hours, or until set. Turn off oven heat and let cake stand in oven 20 minutes longer. Lift cake dish out of larger pan and place on a rack. Let cake cool about 2 hours, or until it reaches room temperature. Invert plate over the cheesecake and carefully turn upside down so cake comes out crumb side up. Slowly spoon syrup over cake. Just before serving, spoon preserves in a narrow ring around outer rim of cake.

Beverages

Strawberry Punch *18 punch-cup servings*

1½ cups cold water
1½ cups Smucker's Strawberry Syrup
2½ cups unsweetened pineapple juice
½ cup lemon juice

1 quart ginger ale, chilled
Red food coloring (optional)
Ice ring or cubes

Pour cold water into punch bowl. Add syrup, pineapple juice, and lemon juice; stir to blend. Just before serving, add ginger ale. Add few drops of red food coloring, if desired. Float ice ring or ice cubes in punch. Serve immediately.

Tangy Raspberry Fizz *8 servings*

1 cup Smucker's Red Raspberry Syrup
1 cup Smucker's Apricot Syrup
1 cup unsweetened grapefruit juice

1 cup cold water
1 quart ginger ale, chilled
Ice cubes

In a pitcher, combine syrups, juice, and water; blend well. Gradually add ginger ale and mix lightly. Serve immediately over ice.

Chocolate Milkshake *1 serving*

¼ cup Smucker's Chocolate Flavor
* Syrup Topping*

⅓ cup milk
1 cup (½ pint) vanilla ice cream

Combine all ingredients in container of blender. Cover and process at medium speed 1 minute. Or combine ingredients in a bowl and beat well with a rotary beater. Pour into a chilled glass and serve immediately.

Mulled Apricot Punch *6 to 8 servings*

3 to 5 whole cloves
1 cinnamon stick
4 cups water

1½ cups Smucker's Apricot Syrup
¼ cup lemon juice
1 lemon, thinly sliced

In a saucepan, combine cloves, cinnamon, and water. Bring to a boil. Reduce heat; cover and simmer 30 minutes. Remove cloves and cinnamon stick. Just before serving, add syrup and lemon juice. To serve, place a slice of lemon in each cup and pour hot apricot punch over. Serve hot.

▼▲▼

Old-Fashioned Tea Punch *12 to 14 servings*

3 cups unsweetened pineapple juice
1½ cups strong cold tea
½ cup Smucker's Apricot Syrup
½ cup lime juice

2 cups ginger ale
Ice cubes
Lime slices
Mint sprigs

In a pitcher, combine pineapple juice, tea, syrup, and lime juice. Refrigerate to chill thoroughly. Just before serving, pour into punch bowl. Add ginger ale and ice cubes. Garnish with lime slices and mint sprigs. Serve immediately.

▼▲▼

Mocha Hot Chocolate *4 servings*

3 cups milk
½ cup Smucker's Chocolate Flavor
  Syrup Topping
2 tablespoons instant coffee powder
1 teaspoon vanilla extract

¾ cup water
½ cup heavy or whipping cream,
  whipped
Ground cinnamon

In large saucepan, combine milk, topping, instant coffee, vanilla, and water. Stir until coffee dissolves. Cook over medium heat, stirring frequently, until hot but not boiling. Pour into cups. Top each serving with a spoonful of whipped cream and a sprinkling of cinnamon.

Raspberry Frost   *25 punch-cup servings*

2 cups cold water
1 cup Smucker's *Red Raspberry Syrup*
2 (6-ounce) cans frozen lemonade
 concentrate, thawed

2 quarts raspberry flavor carbonated
 beverage, chilled
Ice cubes
Lime slices

Pour water into punch bowl. Add syrup and stir to blend. Add lemonade concentrate and carbonated beverage, mixing gently. Add ice cubes. Top with lime slices. Serve immediately. (See photo, page 13.)

Mint Sparkle   *8 to 10 servings*

1 cup Smucker's *Mint Flavored Apple*
 Jelly
¾ cup water
2¼ cups unsweetened pineapple juice

½ cup lime juice
1 quart ginger ale, chilled
Ice cubes

In a saucepan, combine jelly and water. Heat, stirring constantly, until jelly is melted. Cool. Add pineapple juice and lime juice; stir to blend. Refrigerate until serving time. To serve, slowly blend ginger ale into jelly mixture. Pour into glasses over ice cubes. Serve immediately.

Quick/Easy Beverage Ideas

Apricot Fizz
In a tall glass, combine 2 tablespoons Smucker's Apricot Syrup and 1 scoop vanilla ice cream. Stir to blend well; fill glass with chilled club soda.

Special Chocolate Soda
In a tall glass, combine ¼ cup Smucker's Chocolate Flavor Syrup Topping and 2 tablespoons light cream. Stir to blend well. Fill glass ⅔ full with chilled club soda. Top with small scoop of vanilla ice cream.

Double Raspberry Float
In a tall glass, combine 2 tablespoons Smucker's Red Raspberry Syrup, 1 scoop raspberry sherbet, and 1 scoop vanilla ice cream. Fill glass with chilled club soda or lemon-lime carbonated beverage.

Index

Appetizer Meatballs, 12
Apple Chutney, 32
Apples, Marmalade-Walnut Baked, 52
Apricot
  Chicken, 24
  Fizz, 59
  Mold, Pat's, 28
Aunt Dilla's Jelly-Icing Cake, 44

Batter-Fried Shrimp, 25
Beef
  Brisket, Glazed, 16
  Sauerbraten, 14
  Short Ribs, Spicy, 16
Beets, Spiced, 31
Berrybush Christmas Cookies, 41
Bread
  Jelly-Glazed Sally Lunn, 34
  Orange Marmalade, 36
  Picture-Pretty, 37
Breakfast Blossoms, 36
Brownie Pie A La Mode, 49

Cabbage, Red, 31
Cake
  Aunt Dilla's Jelly-Icing, 44
  Cheese Sensation, 56
  Downside-Up Cherry, 46
  Jelly Roll, 46
Caramel Flan, 52
Carrots, Glazed, 31
Cheese Dollars, Dressed-Up, 11
Cheesecake Sensation, 56
Cherry-Roasted Chicken, 24
Chicken
  Apricot, 24
  Cherry-Roasted, 24
  Curried Orange, 22

Dunkers' Delight, 12
  Peach-Glazed, 22
Chocolate
  Milkshake, 57
  Mocha Hot, 58
  Soda, Special, 59
Chutney
  Apple, 32
  Plum, 32
Cole Slaw, Orange-Pineapple, 30
Cookies
  Berrybush Christmas, 41
  Grandmother's Jelly, 42
  Grape-Nut Triangles, 41
  Jelly-Nut Thumbprints, 40
  Jennie's Special Ladyfingers, 40
  Sandbakkelse, 42
Currant Roast Lamb, 18
Curried Orange Chicken, 22

Double Raspberry Float, 59
Downside-Up Cherry Cake, 46
Dressed-Up Cheese Dollars, 11
Dunkers' Delight, 12

Fish Sticks, Sweet-Sour, 25
Flan, Caramel, 52
Frozen Strawberry Pie, 56

Glazed Beef Brisket, 16
Glazed Carrots, 31
Grandma's Baked Squash, 30
Grandmother's Jelly Cookies, 42
Grape
  Dessert Sauce, 54
  Lamb Chops, 18
  -Nut Triangles, 41
  Nutted, Sauce, 54
Griddle Cakes, 38

Ham
  Spicy Plum-Sauced, 20
  Steak, Strawberry, 20
Hot Mint Sauce, 32

Ice Cream, Strawberry, 54
Icing, Whipped Jelly, 44

Jelly
  -Glazed Sally Lunn, 34
  -Nut Thumbprints, 40
  Roll, 46
  Sauce, 18
Jennie's Special Ladyfingers, 40

Lamb
  Chops, Grape, 18
  Roast, Currant, 18
  Special Skewered, 17

Marmalade-Walnut Baked Apples, 52
Meatballs
  Appetizer, 12
  Sweet-and-Sour, 17
Milkshake, Chocolate, 57
Mint
  Sauce, Hot, 32
  Sparkle, 59
Mocha Hot Chocolate, 58
Mulled Apricot Punch, 58

Nutted Grape Sauce, 54

Old-Fashioned Tea Punch, 58
Orange
  Marmalade Bread, 36
  -Pineapple Cole Slaw, 30
  Sauce, 26

Pancakes
  Griddle Cakes, 38
  Saucer, 37
  Swedish, 38
Pat's Apricot Mold, 28
Peach
  -Glazed Chicken, 22
  Tarts, 49
Picture-Pretty Bread, 37
Pie
  Brownie, A La Mode, 49
  Pineapple Cheese, 48
  Pumpkin Marmalade, 48
  Strawberry-Cheese, 50
Pineapple
  Cheese Pie, 48
  Spareribs, 20
Plum
  Chutney, 32
  Hot, 26

Pork
  and Peppers, 19
  -Kraut-Apple Skillet, 19
Pumpkin Marmalade Tarts and Pie, 48
Punch
  Mulled Apricot, 58
  Old-Fashioned Tea, 58
  Strawberry, 57

Raspberry
  Fizz, Tangy, 57
  Float, Double, 59
  Frost, 59
Red Cabbage, 31

Sandbakkelse, 42
Sauce
  Grape Dessert, 54
  Hot Mint, 32
  Jelly, 18
  Nutted Grape, 54
  Orange, 26
  Plum Hot, 26
Saucer Pancakes, 37
Sauerbraten, 14
Sausage Balls, Sweet-and-Savory, 11
Shrimp
  Batter-Fried, 25
  Sweet-and-Pungent, 26
Spareribs, Pineapple, 20
Special Chocolate Soda, 59
Special Skewered Lamb, 17
Spiced Beets, 31
Spicy Plum-Sauced Ham, 20
Spicy Short Ribs, 16
Squash, Grandma's Baked, 30
Strawberry
  -Cheese Pie, 50
  Frozen, Pie, 56
  Ham Steak, 20
  Ice Cream, 54
  Punch, 57
Sundae Puffs, 50
Swedish Pancakes, 38
Sweet-and-Pungent Shrimp, 26
Sweet-and-Savory Sausage Balls, 11
Sweet-and-Sour Meatballs, 17
Sweet-Sour Fish Sticks, 25

Tangy Raspberry Fizz, 57
Tarts
  Peach, 49
  Pumpkin Marmalade, 48

Whipped Jelly Icing, 44

Yams Baked in Marmalade Sauce, 30